THIS JOURNAL BELONGS TO

_____

The treasures we find at the beach are all elements of an ocean's story; the shoreline is the introduction where we meet some of its characters and are given clues about its far-reaching communities. When you consider the millions of mollusk shells that tumble to shore, you realize that the world's coastlines are jeweled beyond measure. And yet what we see as we look through reeds and seaweed is only a hint of the world beneath the waves, of how these snails and clams and other creatures survive and interact.

Frank Lloyd Wright, at Sunday breakfasts, sometimes placed seashells before him, and spoke with reverence to those gathered about the animals' design solutions. From the spherical moon shell to the swirling banded tulip, from the glassy, elongated olive to the textured murex, mollusks exhibit an astonishing capacity for variation—they're architects of the sea, building magnificent homes that grow with them.

Beautiful and soothing, these intricate calcium carbonate shells are sculptural works of art. With their fluted ribs, spikes and turreted spires, and sporting stripes, plaids or spots, it's no wonder that they've inspired generations around the world: cowries as currency, scallops as tools, and conchs as trumpets for military and spiritual occasions are but a few examples of their functions.

Whether used to hold your innermost thoughts or to track a life list for seashell hunting, think of this lovely journal as a companion who listens to your dreams and ideas, and keeps them safe for you.

To learn more about shells and their creatures, see *The Beachcomber's Companion: An Illustrated Guide to Collecting and Identifying Beach Treasures* by Anna Marlis Burgard, illustrated by Jillian Ditner (Chronicle Books, 2018).

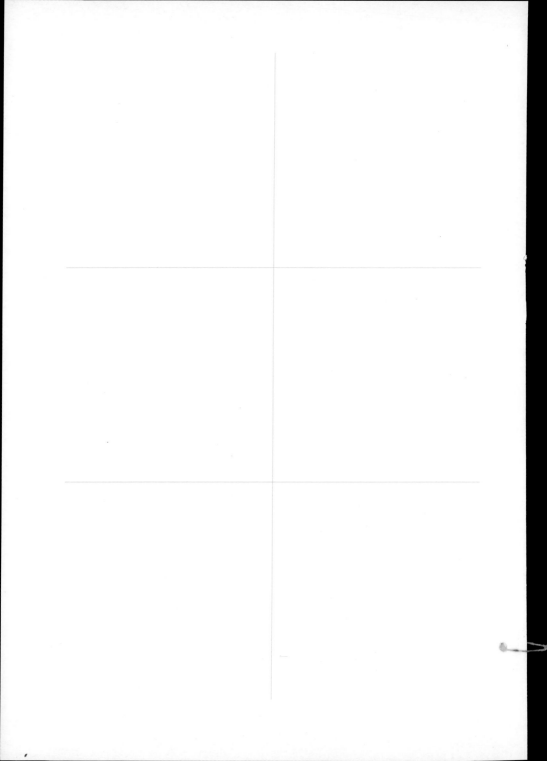

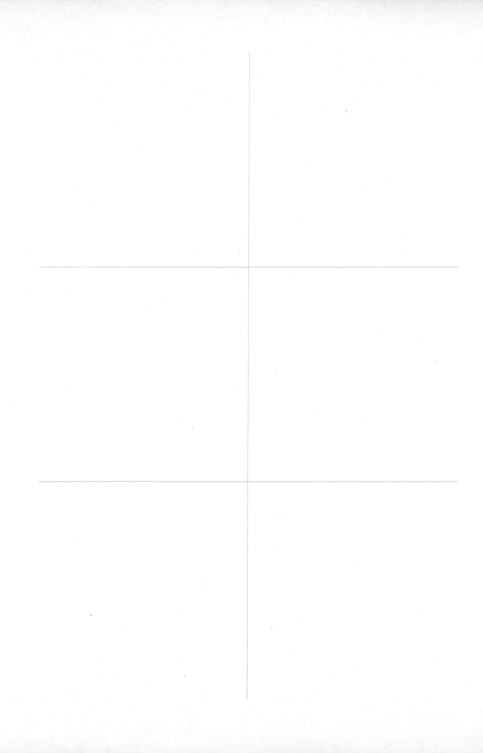

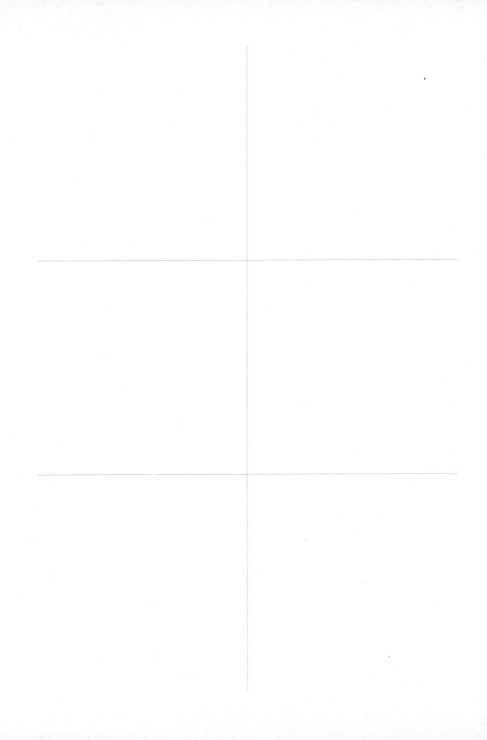

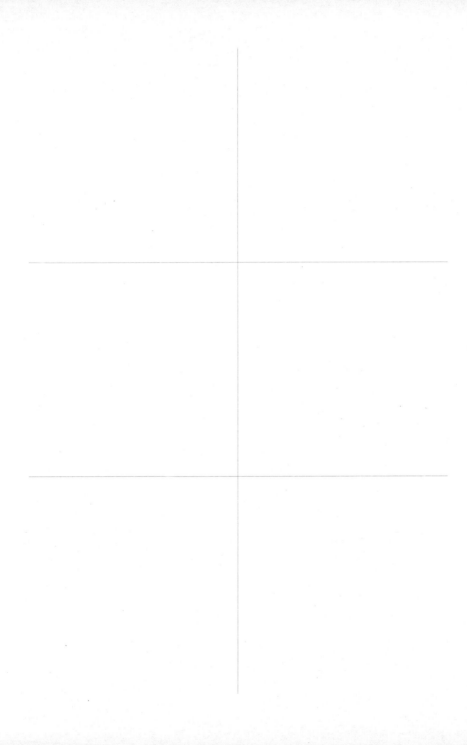

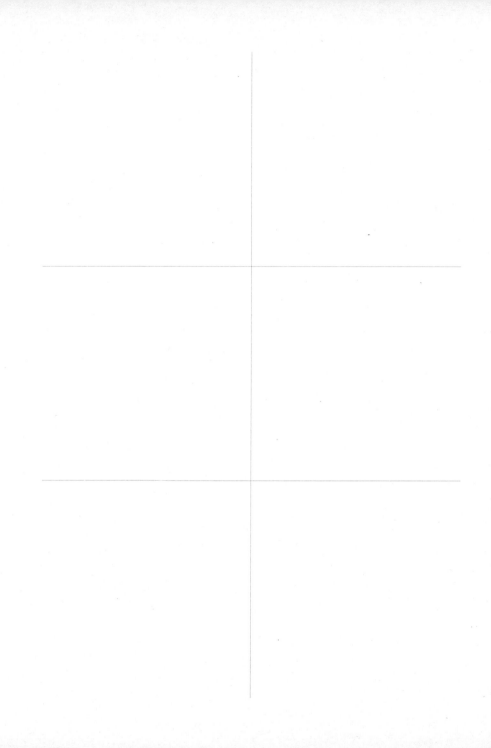

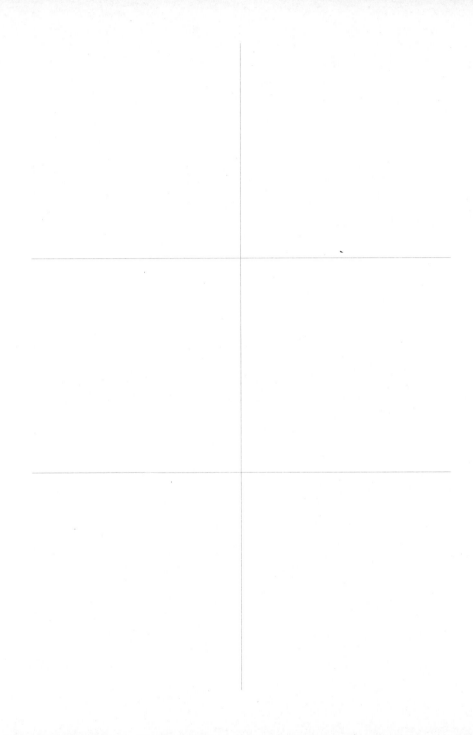

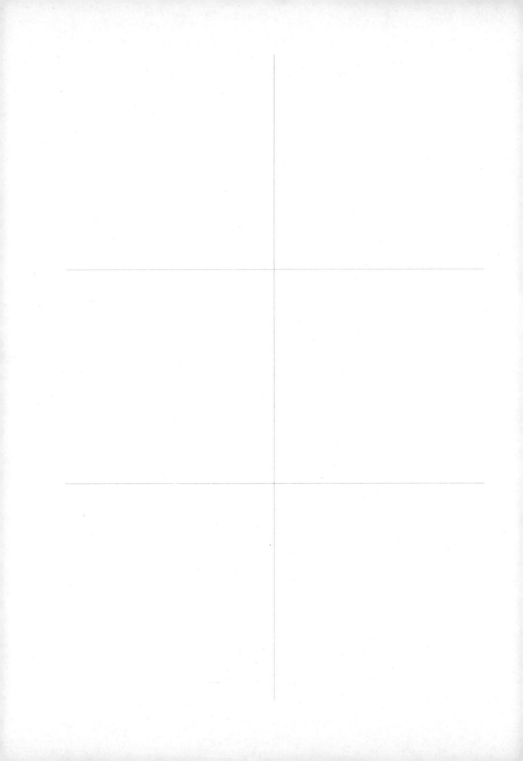

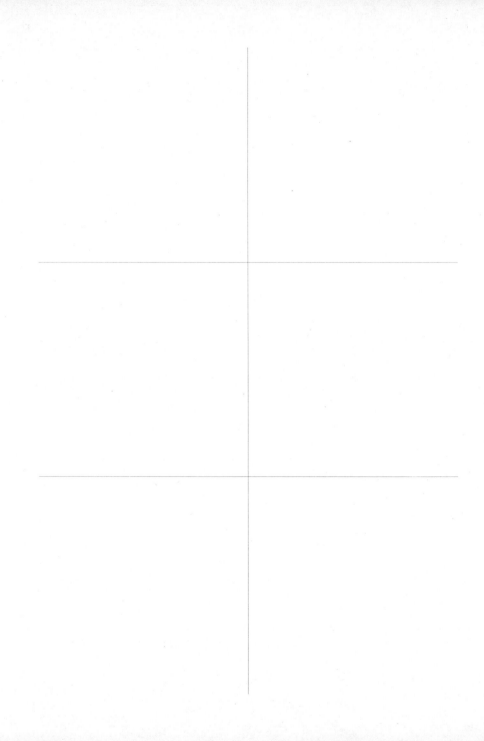

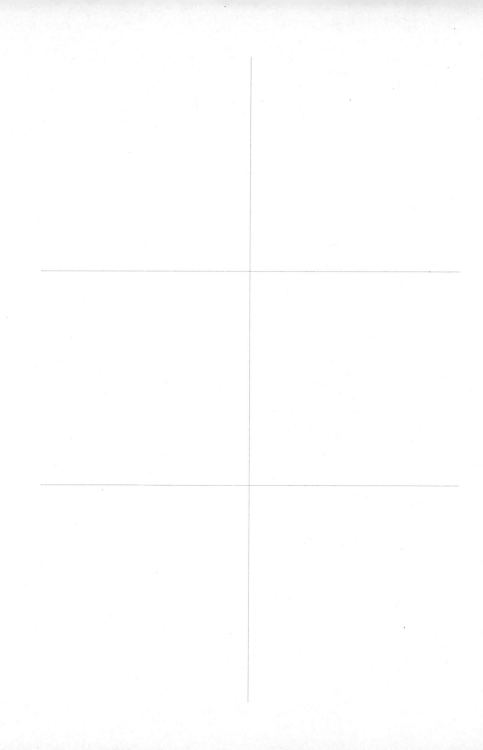

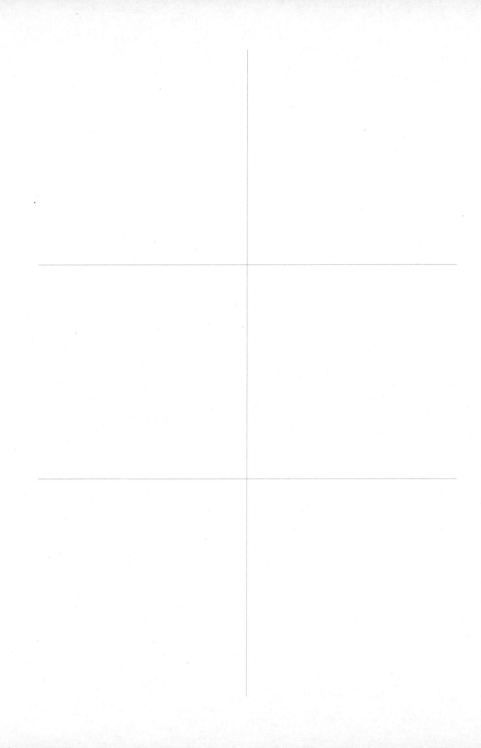

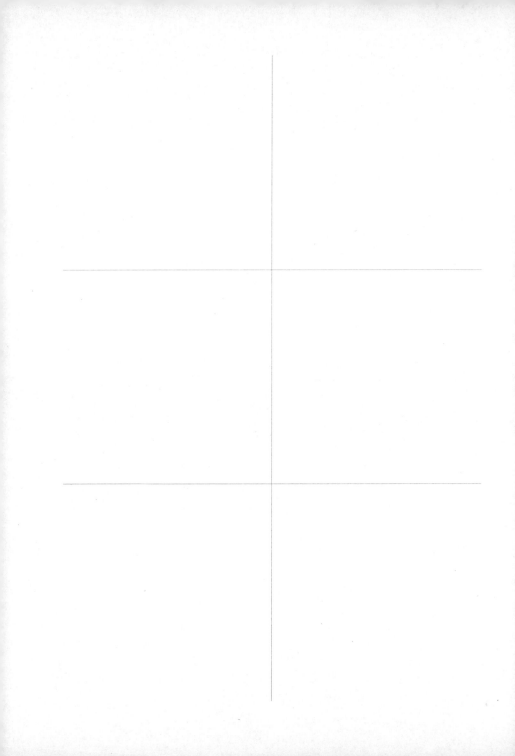

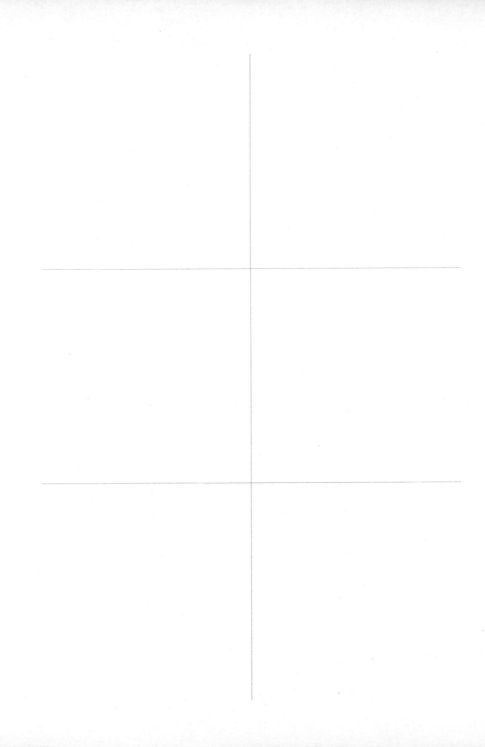

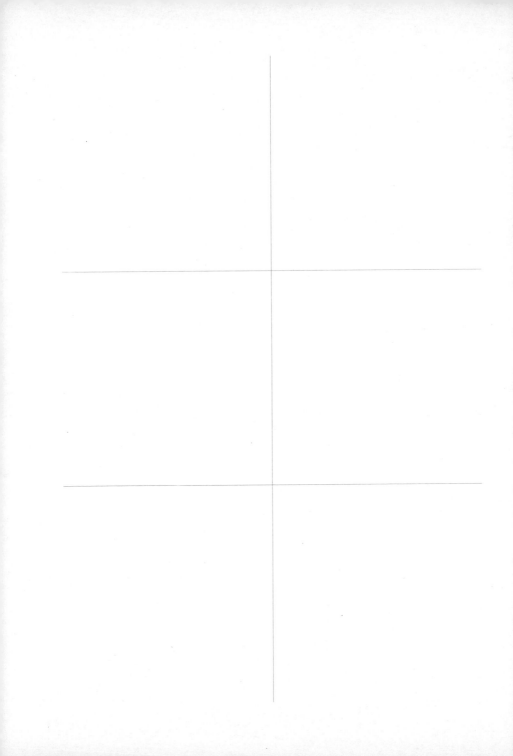

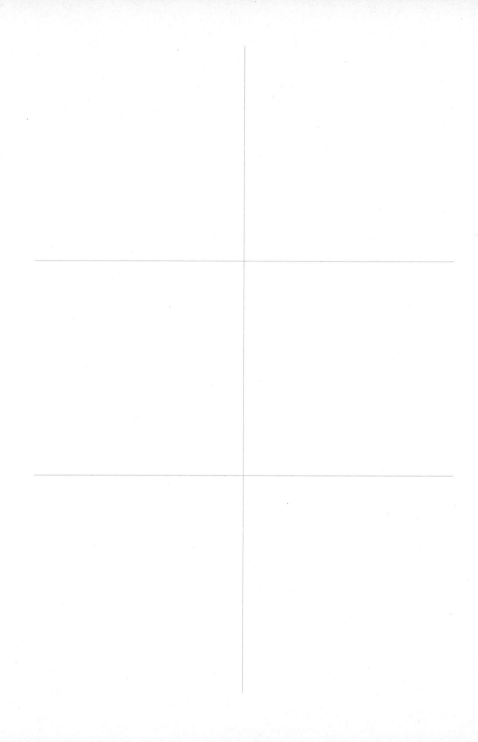

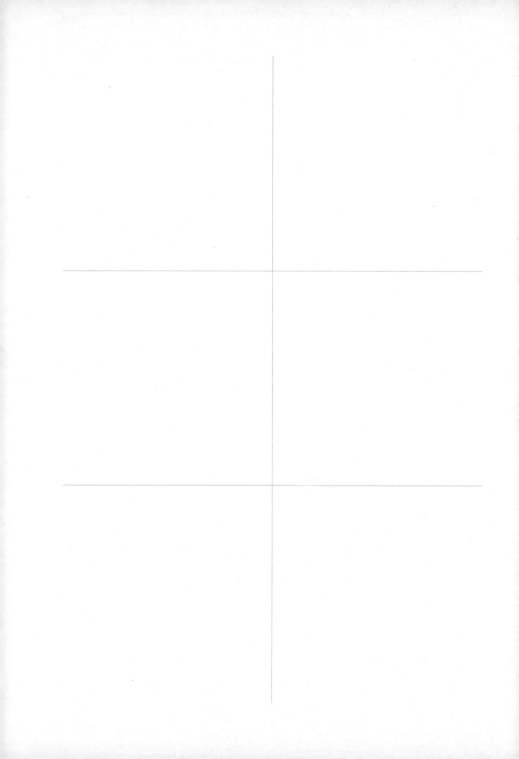

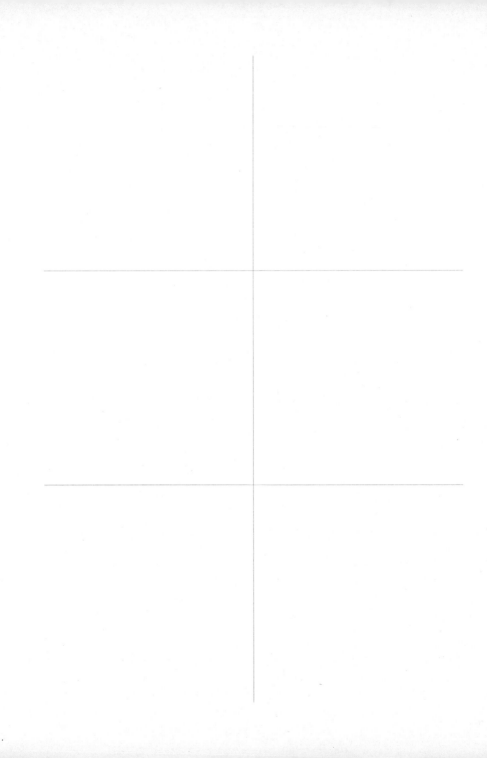

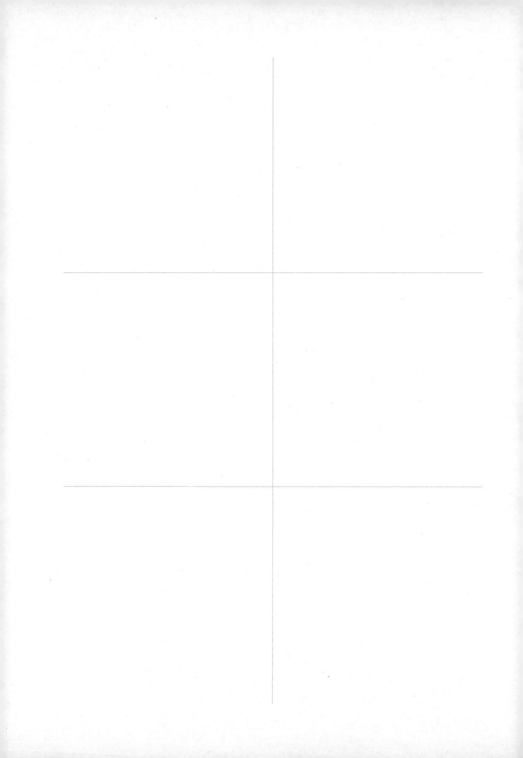

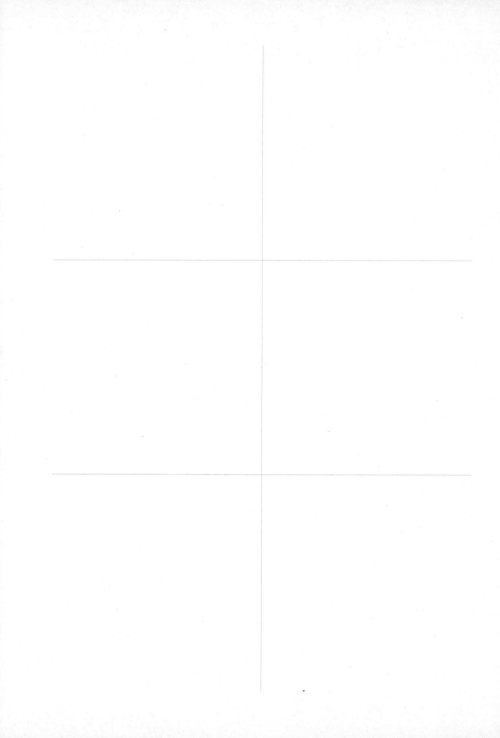

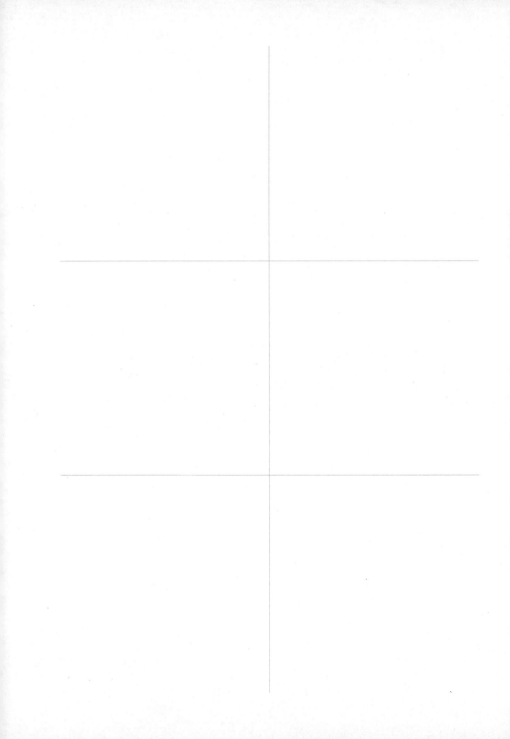

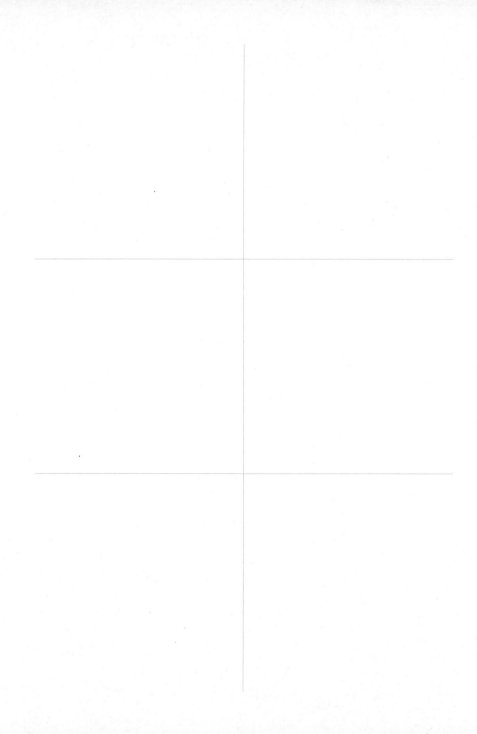